WHAT WE STAND FOR

NO BULLIES ALLOWED!

the kids' book of
DEALING WITH BULLIES

ANDERS HANSON

CONSULTING EDITOR, DIANE CRAIG, M.A./READING SPECIALIST

Super Sandcastle

An Imprint of Abdo Publishing
www.abdopublishing.com

visit us at www.abdopublishing.com

Published by Abdo Publishing, a division of ABDO, PO Box 398166, Minneapolis, Minnesota 55439.
Copyright © 2015 by Abdo Consulting Group, Inc. International copyrights reserved in all countries.
No part of this book may be reproduced in any form without written permission from the publisher.
Super SandCastle™ is a trademark and logo of Abdo Publishing.

Printed in the United States of America, North Mankato, Minnesota
062014
092014

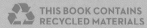
THIS BOOK CONTAINS
RECYCLED MATERIALS

Editor: Liz Salzmann
Content Developer: Nancy Tuminelly
Cover and Interior Design and Production: Anders Hanson, Mighty Media, Inc.
Photo Credits: Shutterstock

Library of Congress Cataloging-in-Publication Data

Hanson, Anders, 1980-
  No bullies allowed! : the kids' book of dealing with bullies / Anders Hanson ; Consulting Editor, Diane Craig, M.A., Reading Specialist.
      pages cm. -- (What we stand for)
  ISBN 978-1-62403-296-7
1. Bullying--Juvenile literature. 2. Bullying--Prevention--Juvenile literature. 3. Aggressiveness in children--Juvenile literature. I. Title.
  BF637.B85H346 2015
  302.34'3--dc23
                      2013041844

Super SandCastle™ books are created by a team of professional educators, reading specialists, and content developers around five essential components—phonemic awareness, phonics, vocabulary, text comprehension, and fluency—to assist young readers as they develop reading skills and strategies and increase their general knowledge. All books are written, reviewed, and leveled for guided reading, early reading intervention, and Accelerated Reader® programs for use in shared, guided, and independent reading and writing activities to support a balanced approach to literacy instruction.

CONTENTS

WHAT IS
BULLYING?

Bullying is unwanted,
forceful words or actions.

Bullies are people who don't feel good about themselves. They bully others because it makes them feel powerful.

Kay gave a wrong answer in class. Ava and Isabel say that she is stupid.

Bullying can be **verbal**, **physical**, or social.

Verbal bullying can be teasing, name-calling, or **threats**.

Physical bullying can be hitting, spitting, or breaking things.

Social bullying can be spreading **rumors**, **excluding** others, or shaming others.

Someone posted a lie about Jordan online. She shows her friend Becky. She knows Becky won't believe the lie.

WHAT CAN
YOU DO?

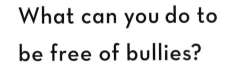

What can you do to
be free of bullies?

STAY IN CONTROL.

You can't control what others do or say. But you can control your own actions. If bullies see you aren't bothered by them, they may give up.

Mariah makes fun of Katie's hair. But Katie likes the way it looks. She doesn't get upset.

WALK AWAY.

If you can, simply walk away from the bully.

If the bully is online, remove him or her from your friend list.

STICK UP FOR OTHERS.

Stick up for people
who are being bullied.
Don't just stand there.

SHARE YOUR FEELINGS.

Tell someone you trust how you feel.
You will feel less sad and angry.

Grace talks to the school counselor.
They meet every Friday.

BE PROUD OF YOURSELF.

Never blame yourself for a bully's actions. Be proud of who you are!

Alan takes dance lessons. Some kids tease him about it. But he doesn't let it stop him from dancing.

WHAT WILL YOU DO?

What is one thing you can do to be free of bullies?

GLOSSARY

EXCLUDE – to leave out.

PHYSICAL – having to do with the body.

RUMOR – a story that is spread around but may not be true.

THREAT – when someone says they plan to harm someone or something.

VERBAL – spoken.